AMAZING ANIMALS

Predators

by Sandra Markle

Illustrations by Jo-Ellen C. Bosson

SCHOLASTIC INC.
New York Toronto London Auckland Sydney
Mexico City New Delhi Hong Kong Buenos Aires

For our good friends Betty and Jim Wass

CAN YOU BELIEVE...

NOTE TO PARENTS AND TEACHERS: This book is intended to help children become aware of the natural process through which food energy is produced by green plants and passed on from one predator to another. Children will also discover that this process renews itself when predators die and decompose, returning to the soil minerals that green plants need to grow and produce food. "All animals depend on plants. Some animals eat plants for food. Other animals eat animals that eat the plants." (National Science Education Standards as identified by the National Academy of Sciences.)

Can you believe

this snake's food energy comes from green plants?

Animals can't produce food inside their own bodies. Only green plants can do that. So animals have to get the nutrients they need to be active and grow from green plants. Some, like this snake, get their **nutrients** from eating other animals that have eaten green plants, or animals that have eaten the green-plant-eaters. Those animals are called **predators**, and the animals they catch are their **prey**. How do predators catch their prey? This book will help you find out. You'll also investigate some special features predators have to help them find their food. Along the way, you'll discover lots of amazing facts about predators—some may even seem unbelievable!

How does a predator find its prey?

A. The predator hunts it down.
B. The predator has it delivered.
C. The predator goes to the store.

Turn the page and start exploring to find out!

Can you believe

an eagle hunts with its eyes?

Like you, an **eagle** sees because light hits light-sensitive cells at the back of the eyes. These cells send messages to the brain. Also, like you, eagles have two forward-facing eyes. (Some animals have one eye on each side of their head, which means they can't look at the same object with both eyes at once.) So the brain receives two sets of overlapping messages. When it analyzes these messages, the eagle gets a three-dimensional image of the world. That lets it judge how far away something is. That way, the eagle can pinpoint the exact location of its prey.

TRY IT YOURSELF!

Find out for yourself how seeing with two forward-facing eyes can help you judge the location of your target.

1. Look straight ahead.
2. Cover both of your eyes with your hands.
3. Have a friend stand about three to five feet (0.9 to 1.5 meters) in front of you and hold up a pencil.
4. First, uncover your left eye and look straight ahead.
5. Next, cover your left eye and uncover your right eye. Surprise! The pencil will probably appear to move, since your brain receives slightly different information from each eye.

Where should you reach to touch the pencil? Try this activity again, but this time, uncover both eyes at once. You should feel more certain about where to reach for the pencil.

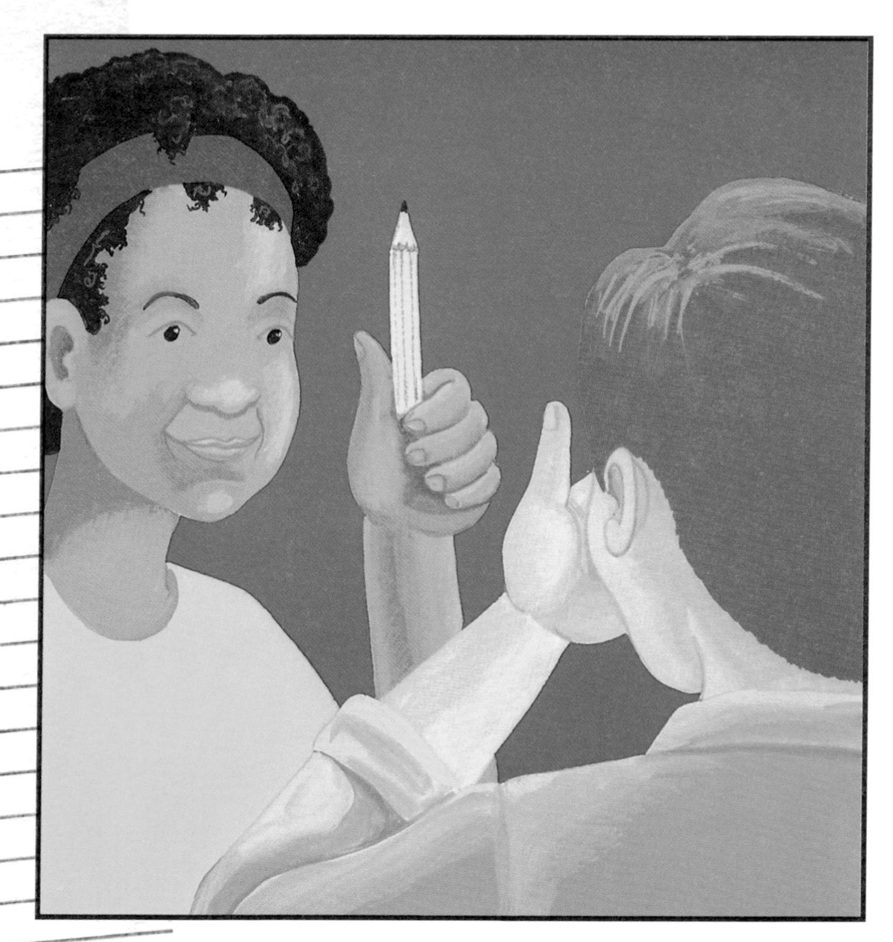

DID YOU KNOW?

An eagle has to turn its head to look up, down, or from side to side. That's because an eagle can't move its eyes in their sockets the way you can.

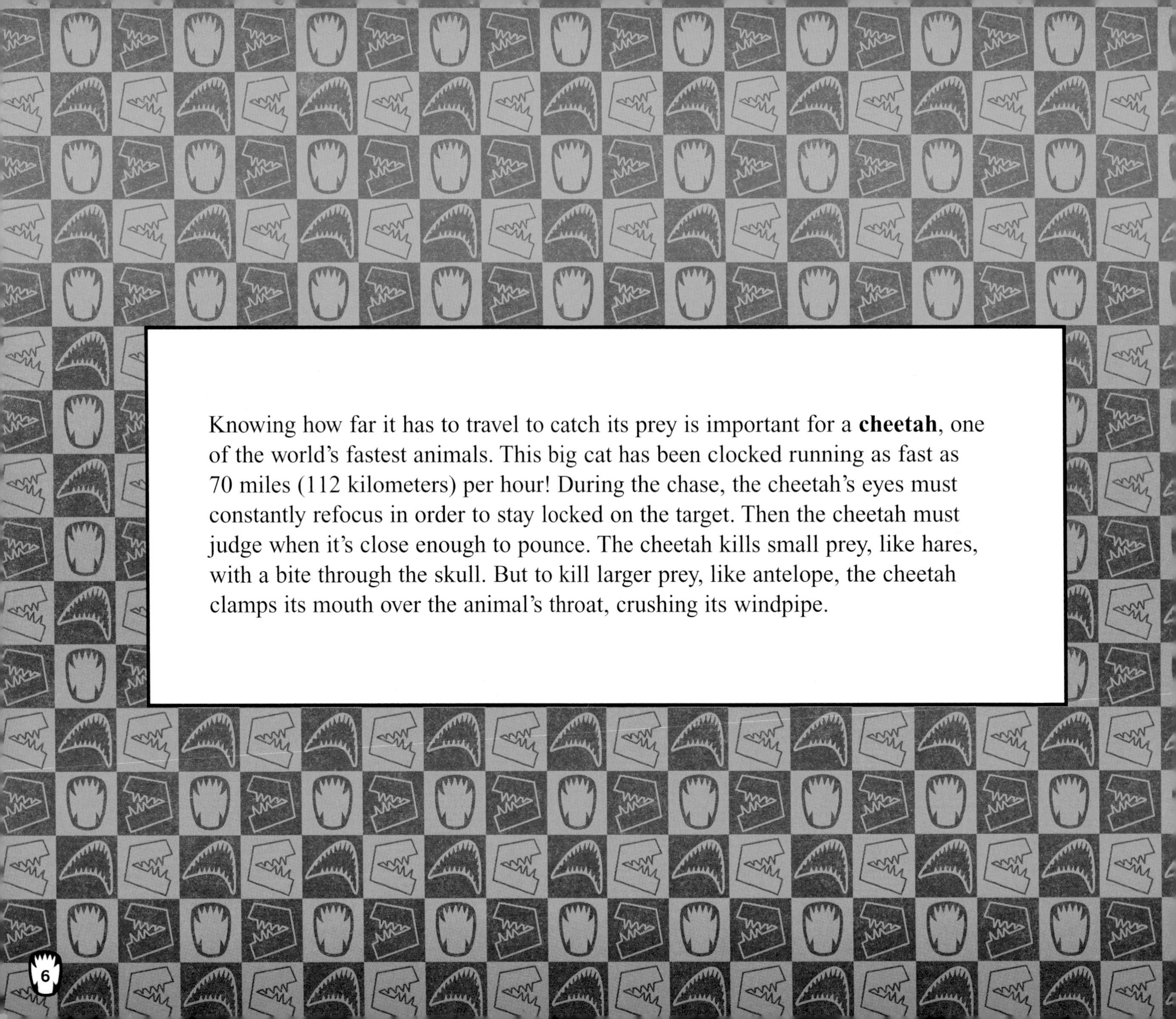

Knowing how far it has to travel to catch its prey is important for a **cheetah**, one of the world's fastest animals. This big cat has been clocked running as fast as 70 miles (112 kilometers) per hour! During the chase, the cheetah's eyes must constantly refocus in order to stay locked on the target. Then the cheetah must judge when it's close enough to pounce. The cheetah kills small prey, like hares, with a bite through the skull. But to kill larger prey, like antelope, the cheetah clamps its mouth over the animal's throat, crushing its windpipe.

Many other animals use their eyes to track their prey. To catch a salmon swimming upstream, a **grizzly bear** uses its eyesight to decide when to act. Then, if it's fast enough, the bear can catch a fish in midair.

TRY IT YOURSELF!

How fast can you respond to what you see?

1. Tie a two-foot (60-centimeter) piece of string to a pretzel.
2. Sit on a chair and stare straight ahead.
3. Have a partner stand behind you and swing the pretzel so it passes just in front of your face.
4. As soon as you see the pretzel, try to grab it with your teeth while it's directly in front of you. If you miss, try again.

Did you get better with practice? Young bears mimic their mothers as they learn how to catch fish. The more practice they get, the better they become at catching fish.

This coyote didn't find its prey with its eyes. Which sense did this predator use?

A. hearing
B. smell
C. sight

Can you believe

the coyote smells the deer?

The **coyote** followed its nose until it could see the deer. Once the deer spotted the coyote, it fled. But the coyote chased after it. Sometimes coyotes hunt alone to catch small animals, like rabbits and squirrels. But usually they team up to hunt bigger animals, like deer. The coyotes take turns keeping the prey running until it's too tired to go any farther. Then they attack.

A **great white shark** may pick up a scent trail long before it sees its prey. Swimming pushes water through the shark's nostrils, into areas called nasal sacs. There, smell-sensitive cells detect tiny bits of chemicals, such as **blood**. These chemical messages are sent to the shark's brain.

DID YOU KNOW?

A shark can "smell" as little as five drops of blood in the amount of water it takes to fill an average-size swimming pool.

There are lots of chemicals in seawater, so the shark has to be able to identify ones that will lead it to its dinner. How good are you at identifying scents?

TRY IT YOURSELF!

1. Tear a piece of paper towel into five strips.
2. Soak one strip in each of the following liquids: vinegar, coffee, lemon juice, orange juice, and chicken broth.
3. Squeeze out any excess liquid over the sink.
4. Have a partner number five self-sealing sandwich bags with a permanent marker. Then have your partner place a different scented strip inside each bag.
5. Your partner should record on a separate sheet of paper which scent is inside each bag. Don't look to see which number matches up with which scent!
6. Open the bags one at a time, put your nose close to the opening, and take a deep breath. Write down what scent you think you smell.

How many of the scents were you able to correctly identify? Can you think of a time when you have used your sense of smell to find something?

This vampire bat crept up on the pig in the dark. How did the bat find its prey?

A. It sensed the pig's warmth.
B. It saw the pig's footprints.
C. It was just lucky.

Can you believe
the vampire bat senses its prey's body heat?

The **vampire bat** has special sensors on its nose. These help the bat find animals in the dark. Once a vampire bat reaches its prey, it uses its two sharp front teeth to slice open a shallow wound. Then the bat laps up the blood that flows out. Usually, blood would quickly form a scab at a cut, but special chemicals in the bat's saliva keep the blood flowing.

DID YOU KNOW?

A vampire bat's blood meal is likely to equal 60 percent of its body weight. But vampire bats are so small that that's only about eight teaspoonfuls of blood.

Rattlesnakes also sense their prey's body heat. Just above the snake's mouth are two pits containing heat-sensitive cells. These detect differences in air temperature—even very tiny differences. This lets the snake find a mouse, even in the dark, and judge how far away it is.

DID YOU KNOW?

A rattlesnake's fangs are like needles. They inject **venom**, a liquid poison. This not only kills the prey, it also starts the digestion process—before the snake even swallows its food.

This greater bulldog bat is hunting for insects in the dark. What sense is it using to find its prey?

A. hearing
B. smell
C. taste

Can you believe

a bat hunts by listening to echoes?

Snort, click your tongue, or whistle. These are the same sounds **bats** make through their nose or mouth, but usually the sounds are so high-pitched that humans can't hear them. Some bats also have special flaps of skin on their noses to direct the sounds straight ahead.

The bat then listens for an **echo**—its own sounds bouncing back. By analyzing these echoes, the bat's brain figures out a sort of sound picture. This lets the bat fly through the dark without bumping into trees and other obstacles. The bat also uses the echoes to home in on prey. As the bat gets closer to its prey, it shoots out sounds faster and faster. Once it got close enough, the bat in this photo used its wing to sweep the moth into its mouth.

TRY IT YOURSELF!

Did you guess that the bat's big ears help it hunt?

1. Roll up two sheets of construction paper and tape them to make two funnels.
2. Leave the room, and while you're away have a partner move to an unknown part of the room.
3. Close your eyes and have another partner guide you back into the room.
4. Make loud clicking sounds and have your mystery partner echo these. Can you pinpoint your mystery partner's location?
5. While you keep your eyes closed, have your helper partner hold the two paper funnels up to your ears. Together, slowly turn in a circle. Do your big ears make it easier to locate your mystery partner when he or she echoes your clicks?

TRY IT YOURSELF!

You can also test out your hearing skills with a group.

1. Have a group stand in a circle, with the person playing the bat in the center.
2. Blindfold the bat.
3. Then silently pick someone else to be the moth.
4. Have the bat make a clicking sound.
5. Have the moth echo the bat's sound while everyone else responds with some other sort of sound.
6. After each round of calls, the bat should take a step toward where he or she thinks the moth is.

How many rounds of sounds does it take the bat to catch the moth?

DID YOU KNOW?

When a bat calls out, muscles squeeze its middle ear. This keeps the bat from being deafened by its own sounds. Then the muscles relax so it can listen for the echo.

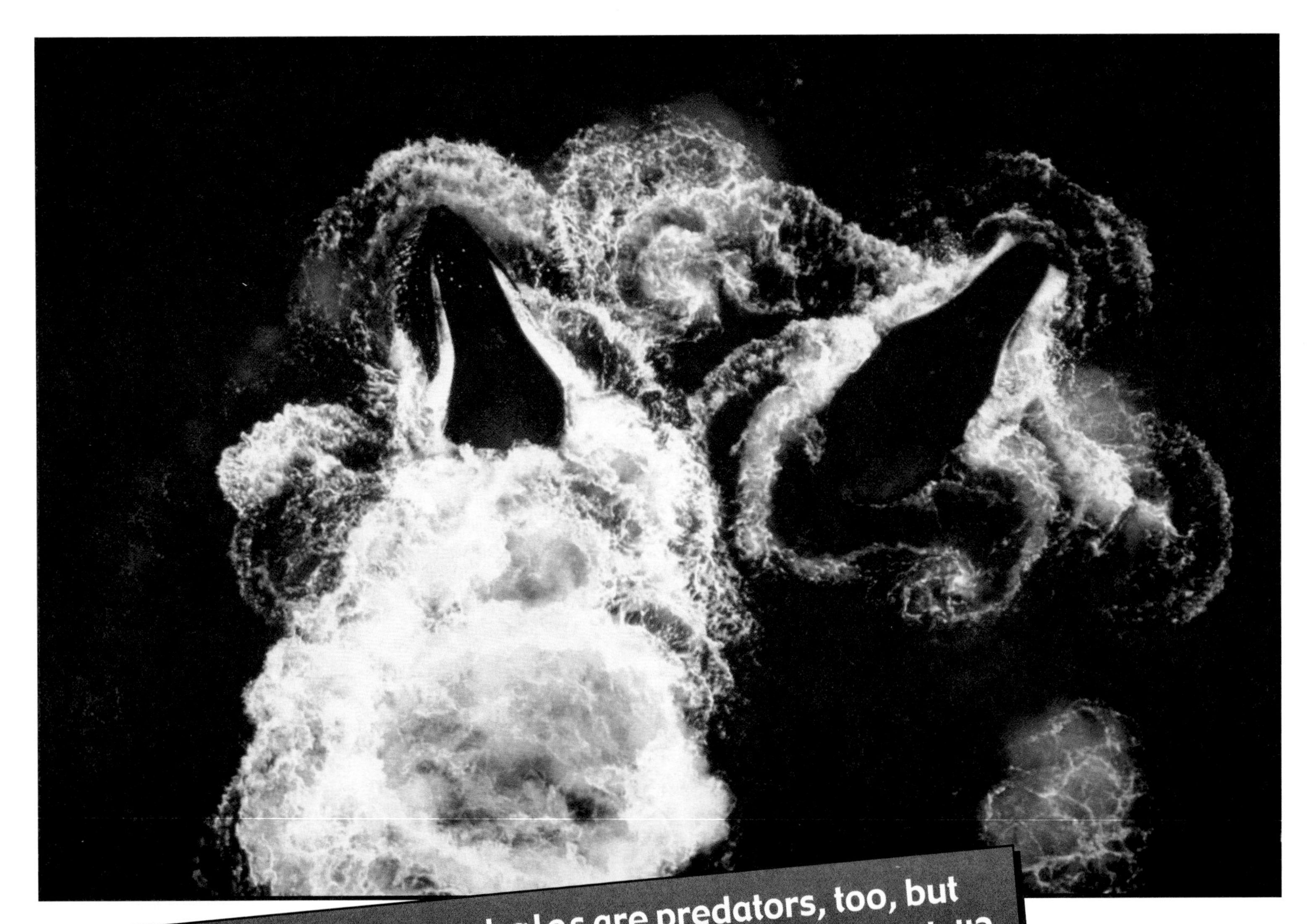

These humpback whales are predators, too, but they're not chasing their prey. How will they catch it?

A. ambush it
B. trap it
C. trick it

Can you believe

humpback whales make a trap?

When a group of **humpback whales** comes upon a school of fish, the whales swim in a circle. As they swim, each whale blows bubbles out its blowhole, the breathing hole on top of its head. These bubbles hang in the water like a net. Most fish become confused and won't swim through them.

TRY IT YOURSELF!

Find out how a humpback whale can trap fish between bubbles!

1. Cut off the top of a clear plastic soft drink container.
2. Drop in some small Styrofoam pieces. These are your "fish."
3. Insert the end of a straw just below the surface of the water and blow into it gently. You'll create a froth of bubbles.
4. Keep on blowing as you move the straw around the "fish," encircling them with bubbles.

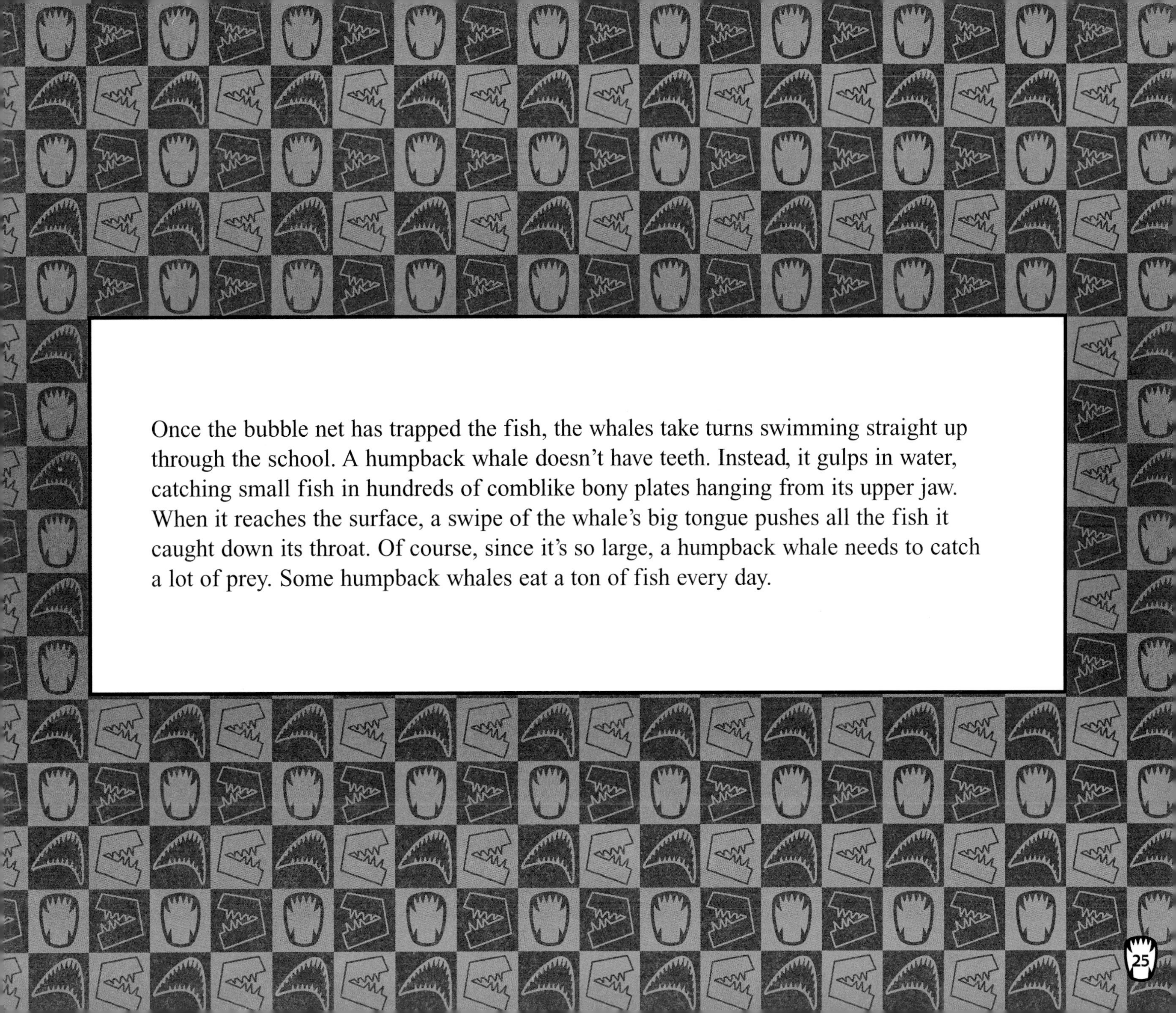

Once the bubble net has trapped the fish, the whales take turns swimming straight up through the school. A humpback whale doesn't have teeth. Instead, it gulps in water, catching small fish in hundreds of comblike bony plates hanging from its upper jaw. When it reaches the surface, a swipe of the whale's big tongue pushes all the fish it caught down its throat. Of course, since it's so large, a humpback whale needs to catch a lot of prey. Some humpback whales eat a ton of fish every day.

Look closely. Do you see the animal that built this trap?

This photo shows the plump, hairy **ant lion**. It digs its pit trap by shoveling with its tail while crawling backward in smaller and smaller circles. Then it hides under the sand in the center of the funnel-shaped pit. If an ant falls in, the ant lion grabs it with its swordlike jaws and sucks out the body juices.

Spiders are champion trap-builders. All spiders produce silk, and some, like the orb web weaver, use it to spin a silk net. To see how the spider constructs its trap, make this model **web**. To really do it the way a spider does, though, you'd need to work at night in the dark. And you'd need to measure the length of each silky strand with your feet!

TRY IT YOURSELF!

1. On the front of a piece of paper, draw two twigs.

2. Use a glue stick to draw a line between the tops of the two twigs. Press a piece of string into the glue. At the end of a night of hunting, spiders usually eat their web in order to store the food energy that's in the silk, but they often leave this top thread intact. It makes starting a new web easier and lets the spider claim a good hunting site as its territory.

3. As shown in the illustration, create two more glued string lines. Connect them from the tops of the twigs to the ground. Then connect the three corners together with smaller glued string lines to create the web's hub.

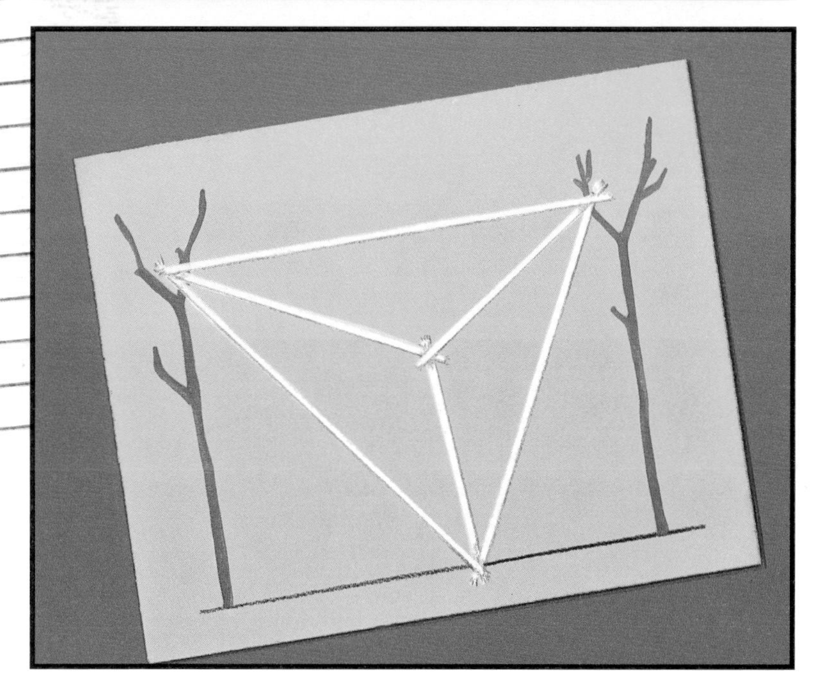

TRY IT YOURSELF!

4. Now add lots of small glued strands, connecting them from the hub of the web to the outer frame.

5. Start at the hub and circle glued strands around and around as you move outward. The spider repeats this step several times, making the web a tightly woven net.

6. To make the web a really good trap, the spider produces an especially sticky silk for the spiral strands of the web. That way, any prey that bumps into the web is likely to get stuck. Place strips of double-sided tape over the strings forming your web's spiral.

7. You may want to add a paper or plastic spider at the web's hub. The spider waits at the center of its web until it feels the vibration caused by something touching its web strands.

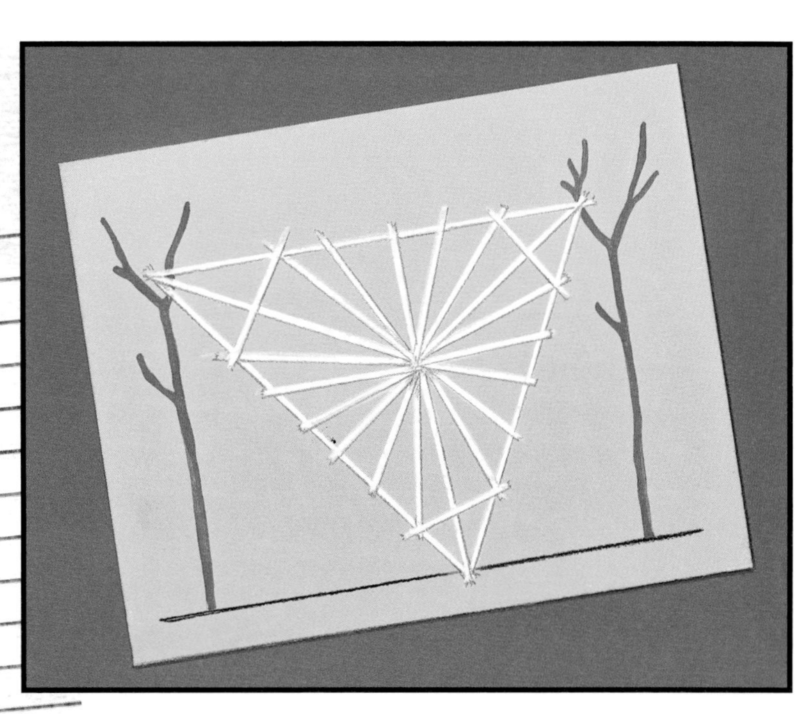

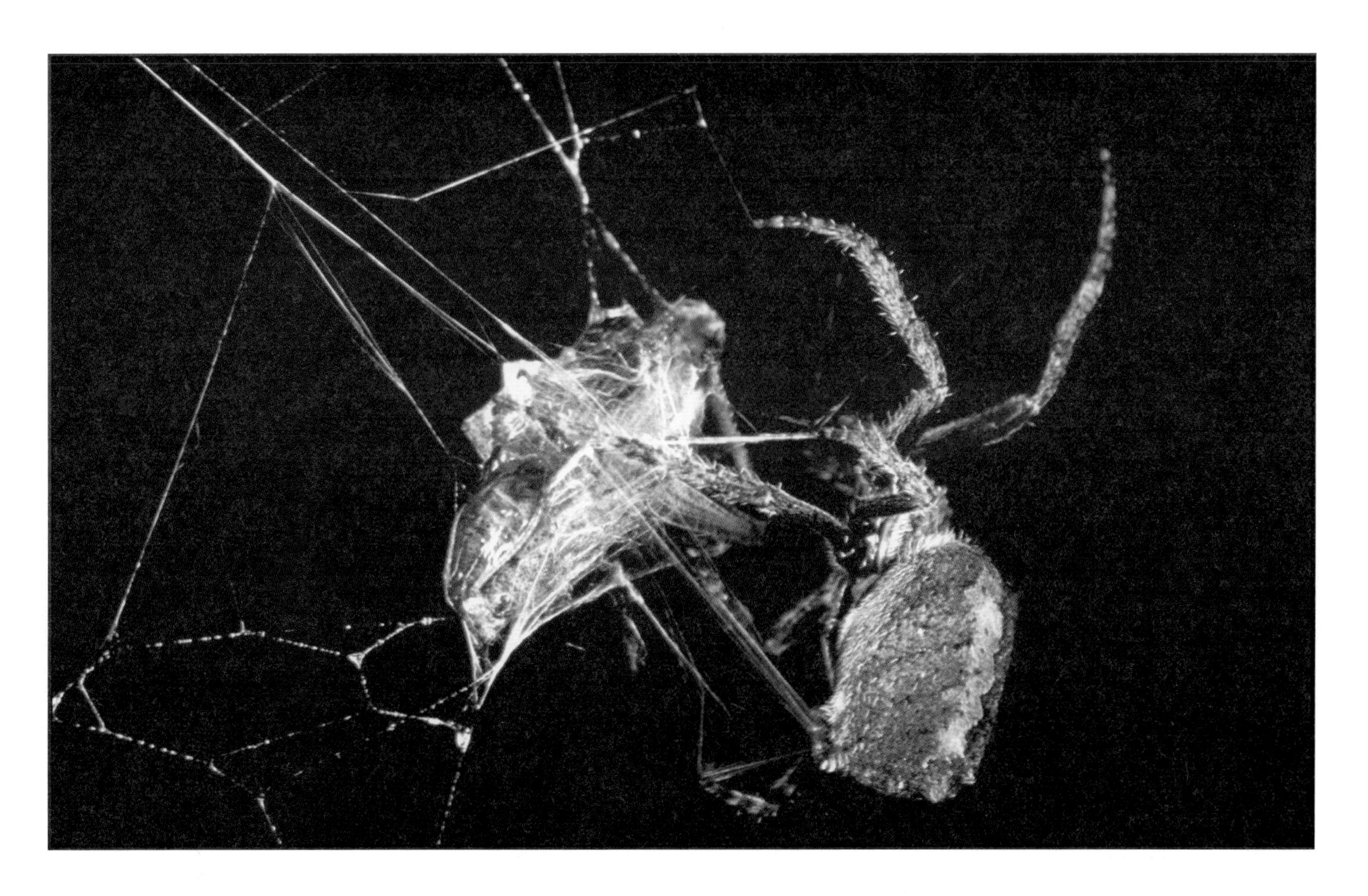

When a cricket landed in this spider's web, the spider rushed to attack it. To keep its prey from struggling enough to break free, the spider sank in its fangs, injecting a little venom. Then the spider quickly wrapped up the cricket in more silk so it couldn't escape. When the spider is ready to eat, it will break open the cricket's tough body with its jaws and bring up special juices from its stomach. Within seconds these juices will dissolve the cricket's soft body parts and the spider will suck in this food.

DID YOU KNOW?

Spiders have taste sensors on their feet. Imagine tasting what you step on!

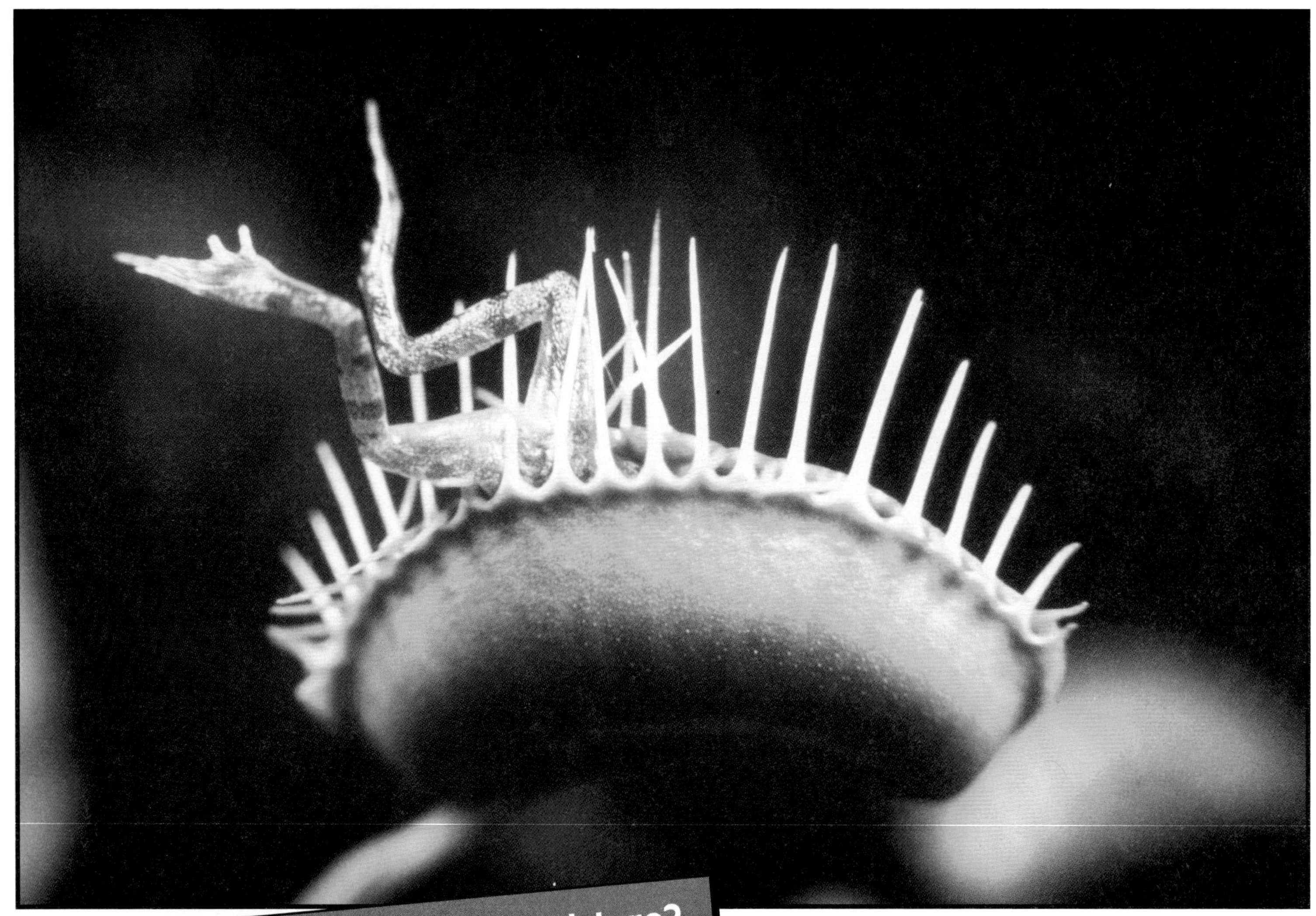

What's happening in this picture?

A. The frog is eating the plant.
B. The plant is eating the frog.
C. The frog is hiding from a predator.

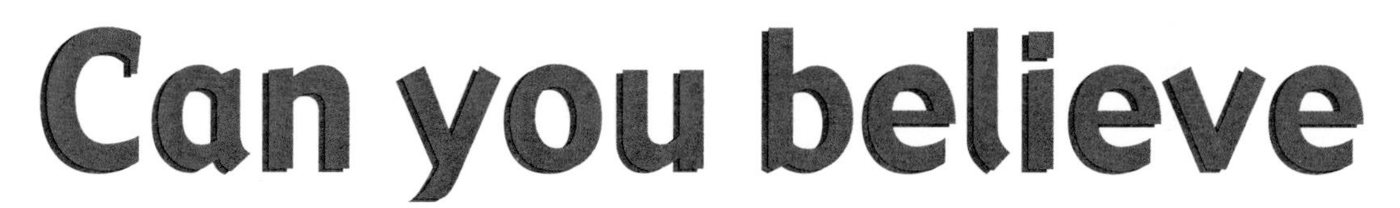

the plant is eating the frog?

Some plants, like the **Venus flytrap**, are predators, too. Like other green plants, these make their own food, but to do that they need certain minerals. They can get these minerals from decomposing animal tissue. That's why these plants can grow in soil too poor to support other green plants.

The Venus flytrap's leaves are traps that snap shut when an insect or tiny frog lands on them, triggering sensitive hairs. Over the next few days, the plant produces special juices that slowly dissolve the animal's soft body parts. The plant soaks up this nutrient soup. Then the trap reopens and the prey's remaining hard body parts are cleared away by rain and wind. After that, the Venus flytrap is ready to catch more prey.

This snake, called an **adder**, is hunting for a lizard dinner. But it isn't using its senses to find a lizard, and it hasn't built a trap to catch one.

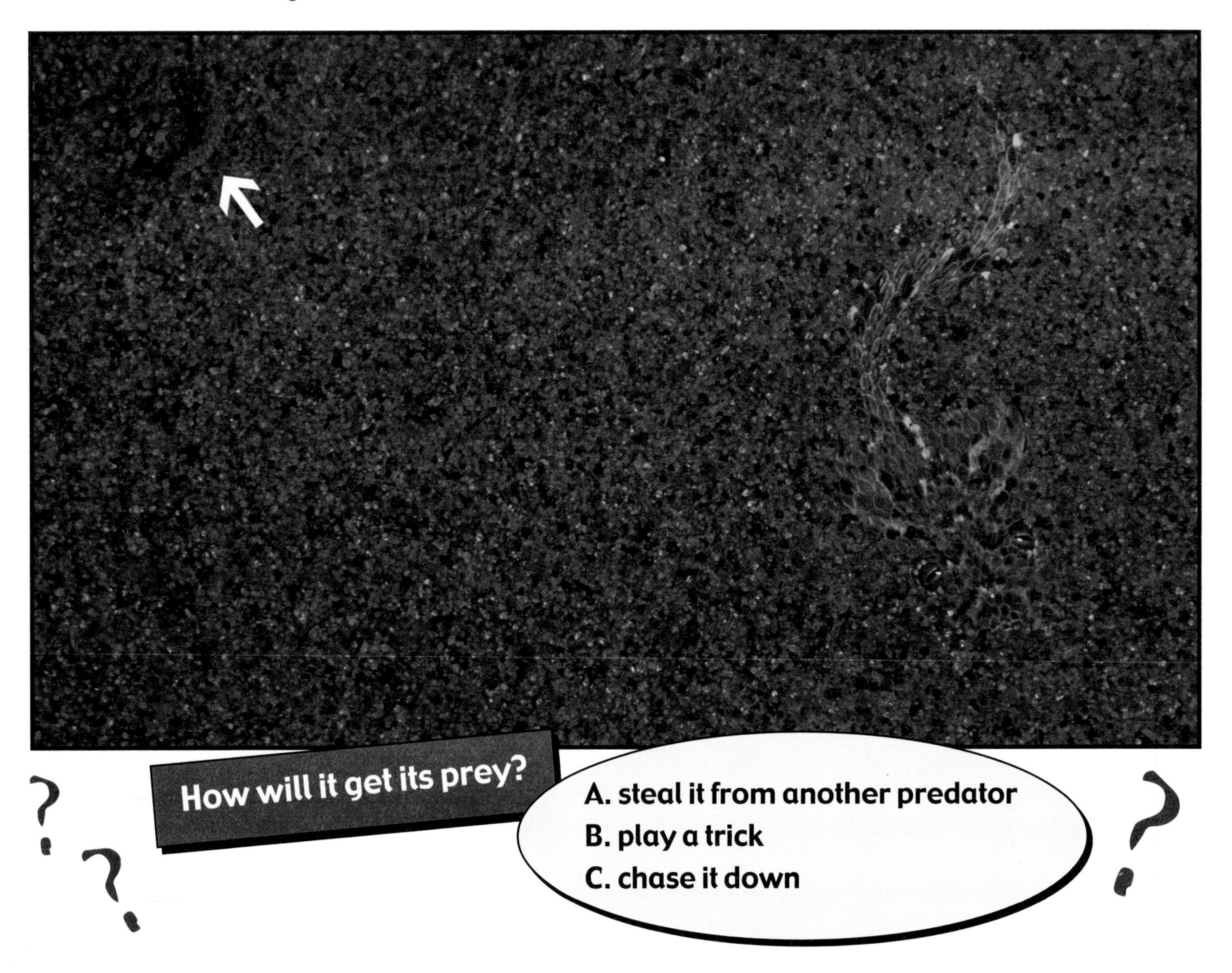

Can you believe

the adder tricks its prey?

Look closely. The adder's skin is colored just right to let it hide in the sand. And its eyes are on top of its head, so it can watch for lizards while it hides. See the tip of the adder's tail sticking out of the sand in the upper left corner? When the adder sees a lizard, it wiggles its tail. Any lizard that tries to catch this little "snake" is likely to end up the adder's dinner.

The **anglerfish** uses a lure, too—a fleshy fin that glows. Like the adder and its tail, the anglerfish can even wiggle this lure to make it more enticing. Did you notice that the lure is just above the anglerfish's wide, tooth-filled mouth? The anglerfish also has a very stretchy stomach so it can gulp down prey nearly as big as it is.

DID YOU KNOW?

Only female anglerfish have a lure. The males are much smaller. Once a male finds a mate, it hangs on, getting its food from the female's bloodstream.

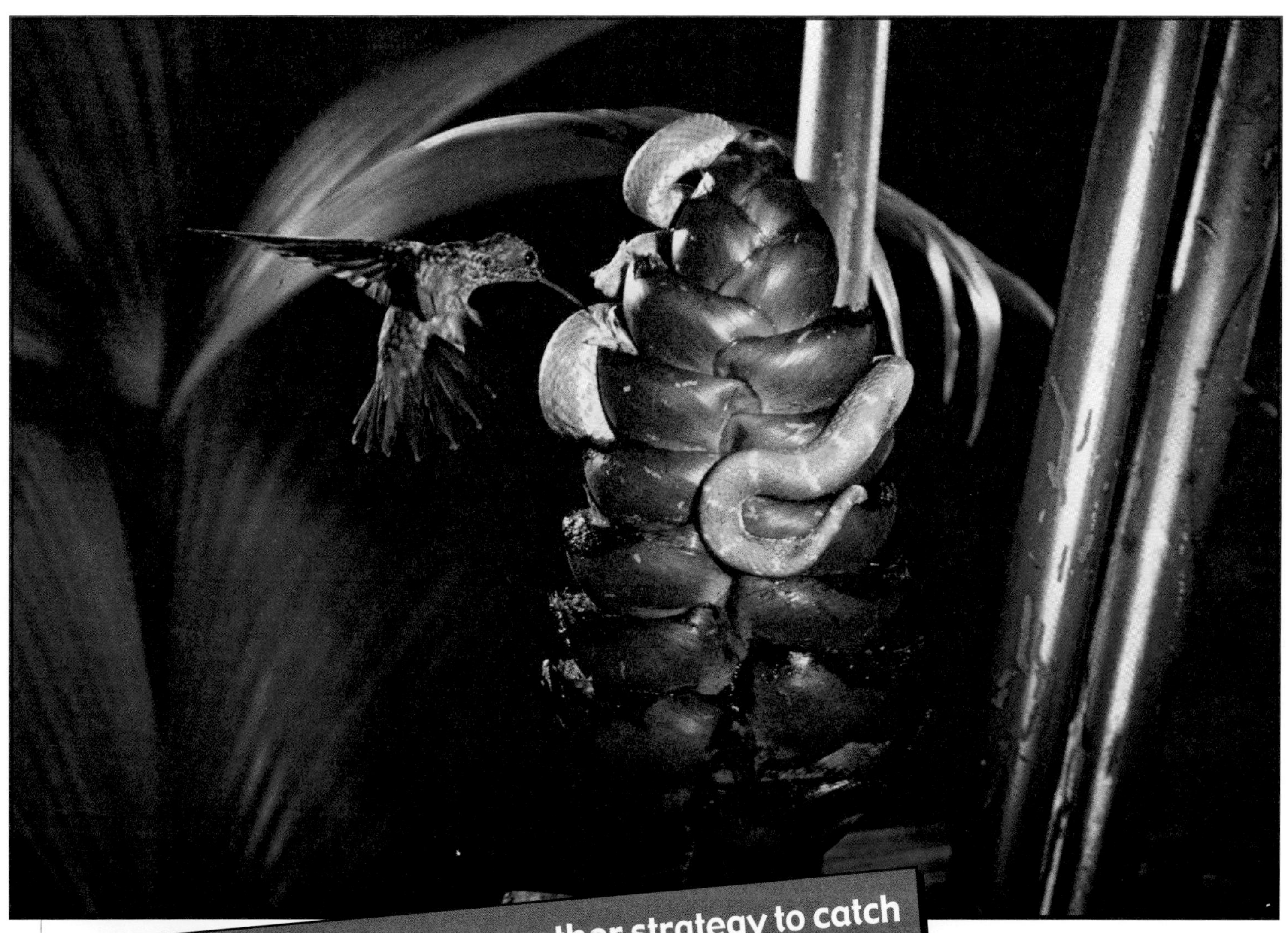

This snake is using yet another strategy to catch its prey. How will it try to catch the bird?

A. chase it
B. shoot venom at it
C. ambush it

Can you believe

the snake ambushes the hummingbird?

Some predators, like this **eyelash viper**, go where their prey is likely to feed. The snake will stay perfectly still and wait. Once its prey arrives, it will lunge, trying to snag it with its fangs.

This time, the snake missed. The hummingbird got away, and the snake coiled up to wait for another chance at a meal.

This **flower mantis** is just the right shape and color to ambush insects coming to feed on flowers. The mantis stays perfectly still until its prey is just within reach. Then it thrusts out its strong front legs, which are armed with overlapping spines. Finally, the mantis bites its prey in the neck to kill it.

Can you believe

a chameleon can ambush prey from a distance?

The **chameleon's** tongue is about as long as its body. Once the chameleon sees its prey, it shoots out its tongue with deadly aim. Not only is the chameleon's tongue sticky, but just before it strikes, the tip twists, creating a suction-cup pad. This gives the chameleon's tongue a super-grip. Then the tongue recoils, carrying the prey into the chameleon's open mouth.

DID YOU KNOW?

A chameleon is able to move each of its eyes separately. That lets it look in two different directions at once, scanning for prey and predators.

Science in Action

Imagine walking through the snow in a dense forest and suddenly coming upon a Siberian tiger. That's what veterinarian Kathy Quigley experienced as part of a team studying these tigers in Russia.

“The tiger looked right at us and roared,” Quigley said. “I could feel the rumble to my bones!” The researchers were in Siberia to learn how to help save the shrinking tiger population. Quigley explained, “We had two goals. First, we wanted to learn everything we could about the tigers and how they lived in the wild. Then we wanted to use this information to create a plan for helping the Siberian tiger population survive—even grow bigger.”

The team accomplished both of their goals. They discovered valuable information about what tigers eat, how large of a home range they cover, how often they have cubs, and how long the cubs remain with their mothers. They also helped the local government understand the importance of setting aside land as a safe home for the tigers.

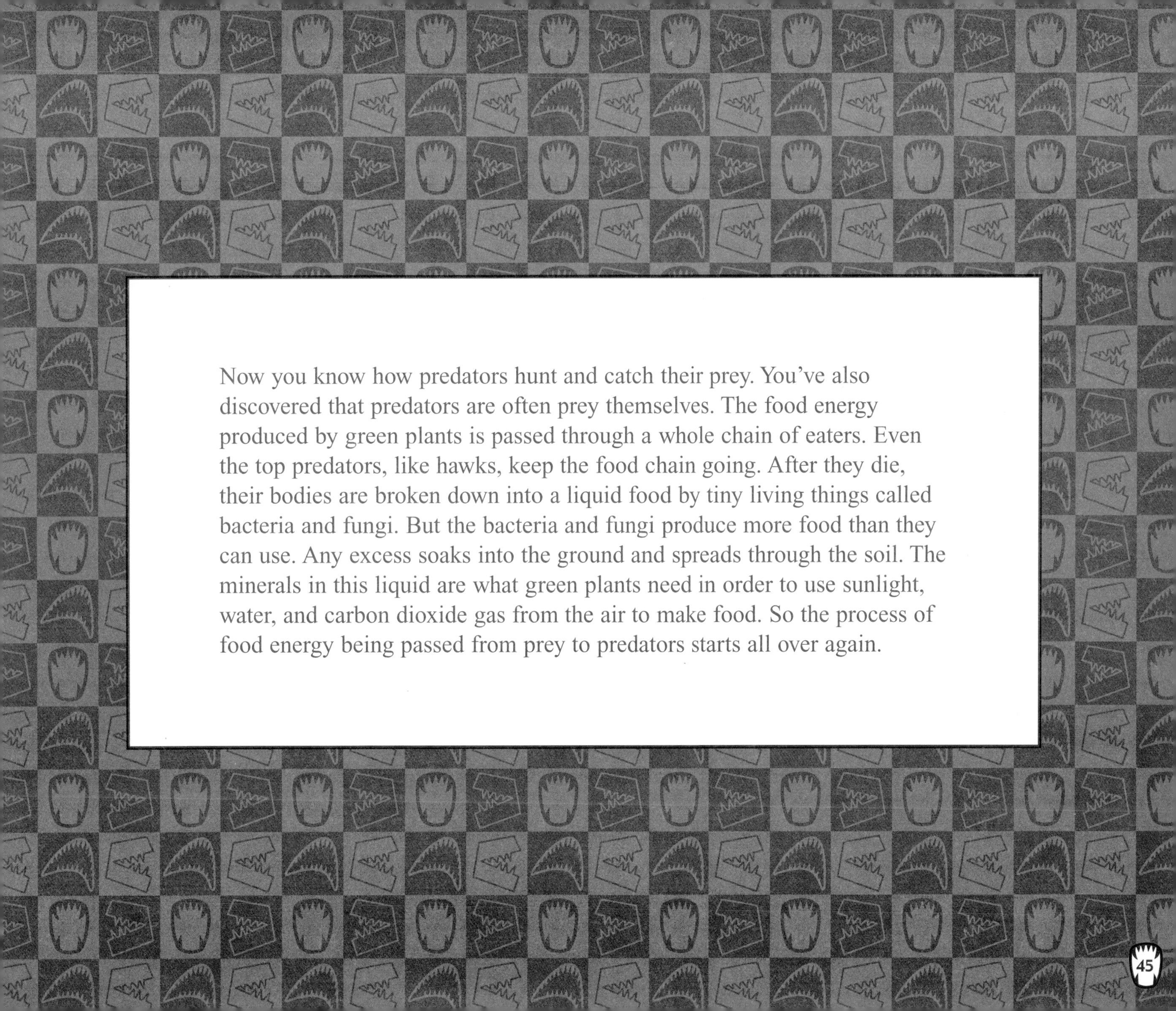

Now you know how predators hunt and catch their prey. You've also discovered that predators are often prey themselves. The food energy produced by green plants is passed through a whole chain of eaters. Even the top predators, like hawks, keep the food chain going. After they die, their bodies are broken down into a liquid food by tiny living things called bacteria and fungi. But the bacteria and fungi produce more food than they can use. Any excess soaks into the ground and spreads through the soil. The minerals in this liquid are what green plants need in order to use sunlight, water, and carbon dioxide gas from the air to make food. So the process of food energy being passed from prey to predators starts all over again.

Glossary/Index/Pronunciation Guide

adder [ADD-er] While there are different types of adders, the one in this book is a Peringuey's adder from South Africa's Namibian Desert. **34-35**

anglerfish [ANG-gluhr FISH] A kind of fish with a slender fin that it uses as a lure to attract prey. **36**

ant lion [ant LYE-uhn] The young, immature form of an insect that looks similar to a dragonfly. It creates a funnel-shaped pit to trap prey. **32-33**

bat [BAT] An animal that uses stretched skin wings to fly in search of food. **17-19**

blood [BLUHD] A liquid in animals that transports nutrients and oxygen to body cells and carries wastes away. **12, 15**

chameleon [kuh-MEE-lee-uhn] A type of lizard found in Africa and Madagascar that uses its very long tongue to catch prey. **40-41**

cheetah [CHEE-tuh] A type of wildcat found throughout Africa, the Middle East, and southwest Asia that is able to run so fast it's considered the fastest land animal. **6**

coyote [kye-OH-tee] Resembling a dog, this predator is found in Central America, Mexico, Canada, and all parts of the United States except Hawaii. **10-11**

eagle [EE-guhl] A type of hunting bird. It often hunts by gliding on air currents while watching the ground for prey. **4-5**

echo [EHK-oh] Sound that bounces back. **19**

eyelash viper [EYE-lash VYE-puhr] This rain forest snake is found in Mexico, Central America, and South America. **37-38**

flower mantis [FLAU-uhr MAN-tiss] One of a number of kinds of praying mantis whose body shape and color help it ambush its prey. **39**

great white shark [GRAYT WHYTE SHARK] A kind of shark with large triangular teeth that have tiny points along the edges like a steak knife—so sharp they can bite through even the toughest-skinned animals. **12-13**

grizzly bear [GRIZZ-lee BAYR] A type of brown bear whose long guard hairs are tipped white or tan, giving it a sort of frosted, or "grizzled" look. **8-9**

humpback whale [HUMP-bak WHAYL] A type of whale that sometimes hunts in a group and eats by filtering small fish and tiny shelled animals out of the water. **25-27**

nutrients [NOO-tree-uhntz] Chemical building blocks into which food is broken down for use by the animal's body. **3**

prey [PRAY] The food a predator catches and eats. **3, 5, 10-13, 16, 19, 21, 23, 29-31, 36, 38-39, 41**

rattlesnake [RAT-uhl-snayk] One of a group of snakes named for the noise its tail tip makes when shaken. **16**

spider [SPY-duhr] A type of insect with eight legs, two main body parts, and the ability to make silk. **30-31**

vampire bat [VAM-pyre BAT] A kind of bat found from Mexico to Argentina and Chile that drinks its prey's blood. **14-15**

venom [VEHN-uhm] Liquid poison used by some predators to help them catch their food. **16**

Venus flytrap [VEE-nuhs FLY-trap] A kind of plant that gets some of the minerals it needs from animals it traps. **28-29**

web [WEB] Silk trap woven by some spiders. **30-31**

PHOTO CREDITS:

Cover: (top left) Art Wolfe; (middle left) C&M Fallons/ Innerspace; (bottom left) Tom and Pat Leeson; (right) Thomas Mangelson/Minden

p. 3: Michael and Patricia Fogden
p. 4: Tom and Pat Leeson
p. 7: Mitsuaki Iwago/Minden
p. 8: Thomas Mangelson/Minden
p. 10: Art Wolfe
p. 12: C&M Fallons/Innerspace
p. 14: Stephen Dalton/Oxford Scientific Films
p. 15: Michael and Patricia Fogden
p. 16: Michael and Patricia Fogden
p. 17: Frans Lanting/Minden
p. 18: Stephen Dalton/Oxford Scientific Films
p. 22: Mitsuaki Iwago/Minden
p. 23: Duncan Murrell/Innerspace
p. 26: James H. Robinson/Animals Animals
p. 27: James H. Robinson/Animals Animals
p. 28: Skip Jeffery
p. 31: Simon Pollard
p. 32: Sean Morris/Oxford Scientific Films
p. 34: Michael and Patricia Fogden
p. 35: Michael and Patricia Fogden
p. 36: Fred Bavendam/Minden
p. 37: Michael and Patricia Fogden
p. 38: Michael and Patricia Fogden
p. 39: Michael and Patricia Fogden
p. 40: Dwight Kuhn
p. 42: Kathy Quigley
p. 43: Kathy Quigley

Acknowledgments: The author would like to thank the following for sharing their expertise and enthusiasm: Paul Broady, Professor, Biology Department, University of Canterbury; Kathy Quigley, D.V.M., Hornocker Wildlife Institute; and Ron Tilson, Director of Conservation, Minnesota Zoo. As always, a special thanks to Skip Jeffery for his help, support, and creative input.

ISBN 0-439-35615-6

Published by Scholastic Inc., 557 Broadway, New York, NY 10012.
SCHOLASTIC and associated logos are trademarks and/or registered trademarks of Scholastic Inc.

12 11 10 9 8 7 6 5 4 3 3 4 5 6 7 8/0

Printed in the U.S.A.
First printing, February 2003